OUR POST-SOVIET HISTORY UNFOLDS

Our
Post-Soviet
History
Unfolds

Eleanor Lerman

Sarabande Books
LOUISVILLE, KENTUCKY

Managing Editor
Sarabande Books, Inc.
2234 Dundee Road, Suite 200
Louisville, KY 40205

Library of Congress Cataloging-in-Publication Data

Lerman, Eleanor, 1952–
Our post-Soviet history unfolds : poems / by Eleanor Lerman.— 1st ed.
          p.   cm.
ISBN 1-932511-24-5 (pbk. : alk. paper)
I. Title.
PS3562.E67O97 2005
811'.54—dc22   2004030201

13-digit ISBN: 978-1-932-51124-6

Cover and text design by Charles Casey Martin

Printed in Canada
This book is printed on acid-free paper.

Sarabande Books is a nonprofit literary organization.

NATIONAL
ENDOWMENT
FOR THE ARTS

This project is supported in part by an award from the
National Endowment for the Arts. Funding has also been
provided by The Kentucky Arts Council, a state agency in
the Education, Arts and Humanities Cabinet, with support
from the National Endowment for the Arts.

TABLE OF CONTENTS

•

II.

ACKNOWLEDGMENTS

•

"Timeless Canyon" and "The Magellanic Clouds" appeared in *Coelacanth Magazine*, Spring 2002.

"Our Post-Soviet History Unfolds," "Living with the Red Menace," "Tales of the Mohawk Valley," "The Drought Summer," "Mountain Lakes," and "Sunset Hammers" appeared in *The Drunken Boat*, Spring 2002.

"About Patti Boyd and Me" is adapted from "About Bob, Patti Boyd, and Me," which won *Wind* magazine's Joy Bale Boone Award in 2002.

I

That Sure Is My Little Dog

Yes, indeed, that is my house that I am carrying around
on my back like a bullet-proof shell and yes, that sure is
my little dog walking a hard road in hard boots. And
just wait until you see my girl, chomping on the chains
of fate with her mouth full of jagged steel. She's damn
ready and so am I. What else did you expect from the
brainiacs of my generation? The survivors, the nonbelievers,
the oddball-outs with the Cuban Missile Crisis still
sizzling in our blood? Don't tell me that you bought
our act, just because our worried parents (and believe me,
we're nothing like them) taught us how to dress for work
and to speak as if we cared about our education. And
I guess the music fooled you: you thought we'd keep
the party going even to the edge of the abyss. Well,
too bad. It's all yours now. Good luck on the ramparts.
What you want to watch for is when the sky shakes
itself free of kites and flies away. Have a nice day.

Starfish

This is what life does. It lets you walk up to
the store to buy breakfast and the paper, on a
stiff knee. It lets you choose the way you have
your eggs, your coffee. Then it sits a fisherman
down beside you at the counter who says, *Last night,
the channel was full of starfish.* And you wonder,
is this a message, finally, or just another day?

Life lets you take the dog for a walk down to the
pond, where whole generations of biological
processes are boiling beneath the mud. Reeds
speak to you of the natural world: they whisper,
they sing. And herons pass by. Are you old
enough to appreciate the moment? Too old?
There is movement beneath the water, but it
may be nothing. There may be nothing going on.

And then life suggests that you remember the
years you ran around, the years you developed
a shocking lifestyle, advocated careless abandon,
owned a chilly heart. Upon reflection, you are
genuinely surprised to find how quiet you have
become. And then life lets you go home to think
about all this. Which you do, for quite a long time.

Later, you wake up beside your old love, the one
who never had any conditions, the one who waited
you out. This is life's way of letting you know that
you are lucky. (It won't give you *smart* or *brave*,
so you'll have to settle for lucky.) Because you
were born at a good time. Because you were able
to listen when people spoke to you. Because you
stopped when you should have and started again.

So life lets you have a sandwich, and pie for your
late night dessert. (Pie for the dog, as well.) And
then life sends you back to bed, to dreamland,
while outside, the starfish drift through the channel,
with smiles on their starry faces as they head
out to deep water, to the far and boundless sea.

Offshore

Ah love. With its taste of candy and wood, smoke in the
afternoon; its Caribbean moods and yellow dresses—still
it knows so little of who we really are. The time has passed
for kisses and courtship, for the innocence of the shoreline:
kicking the little waves, laughing in a swimsuit with the
little skirt. That was a mid-century movie. That was a
        summer carousel. A dream.

Hold a shell to your ear and a ghost will whisper to you,
a ghost of the ocean, of the horizon. The time has passed
for drinks on the patio, for the easy life. Love has taken
all the money and flown off to an island; love is sleeping
with a girl. And love has left us here, in this empty place,
with our empty refrigerators, empty history, forced to
build the same country over and over again. I'm tired
        of it. Aren't you?

Remember when we lived offshore and had every
hope of paradise? Now love doesn't even write to
us with its soft, buttery hand. We wouldn't want to
hear its old lies anyway. Time is short and we—the
ones who can bear to go on living—still have our
        own work to do.

The Magellanic Clouds

In the age of discovery, the Large Magellanic Cloud was already
   visible
        to the naked eye.
It presided over tragic ocean voyages and massacres, the
   destruction of
libraries and temples, ritual burials and the uneven exchange of
   goods.
Looking through his spyglass, Magellan himself thought it had a
        heart-breaking quality
though his was just a feeling. Later, scientists were able to tell us
that the problem with the Large Magellanic Cloud is the Tarantula
   Nebula.
Measurements indicate that this nebula is actually the core of the
Large Magellanic Cloud even though it appears to be off-center
from the rest of the galaxy. Ah. Always off-kilter, pursuing
        its own heart,
the Large Magellanic Cloud hugs the horizon but lurks around all
   night
Sometimes the Large Magellanic Cloud experiences light and
   goodness,
        but more often than not
it knows nothing but trouble. It is pierced by comets. It is
in a transition state and grows bigger and more unwieldy every day.

But there is hope! The Large Magellanic Cloud has a companion,
        a little twin called the Small Magellanic Cloud.
On photographic plates it sometimes appears blurry but believe me,
        it is there.
It may be hard to see, but it has a kind and spiritual nature.
The Russians have been studying it since the Revolution.
Nixon thought about it a lot, so do people who believe that
        their airplane is about to crash.
Who else thinks about the Small Magellanic Cloud?
People who have problems in their love life and their work
(I, for instance, have had it on my mind for years).
The Small Magellanic Cloud knows about our disappointments
        and it sympathizes.
It worries for us sometimes, so we can sleep. But the
Small Magellanic Cloud, whose inner heart is perfectly centered,
        always perseveres.
It follows after the Large Magellanic Cloud and picks up the pieces.
Loving us, loving us, loving us, the Small Magellanic Cloud
puzzles the astronomers because it seems to have no purpose.
But we know better. We whisper its name to our children so they
        may be comforted.
We tell them that every day, stars are born in the Small
        Magellanic Cloud
and then spin off into the universe, remembering us, wishing us well.

Muons Are Passing Through You

This is what is: You are walking down an empty road
in the middle of the night. The poor moon drips
weak light on you like waxy tallow, and it makes you cold.
Your lover has informed you that your services are
no longer needed and your heart feels like a cancer,
your own soul is like a thorn you have been stabbed with.
Dark hedges line the road and there are voices
whispering within them: They are the voices of the
lost, the damned, the many who will be legion.
And they know your name.

And this is true: You are a stardust person.
Muons are passing through you as you read this.
Cosmic rays are building you up and breaking you down.
Seas are evaporating, gases are freezing into planets,
planets are spinning off into the void.
Hold out your hand and watch the pions dance,
watch your nuclei exchanging forces with the universe,
watch the miracles ebb and flow as endless joy
folds into endless silence and everything is
everywhere all at once and it goes on and on.

And here is more: The infinite is already in you.
It is in you and of you, and it may save you.
But if it saves you, it will give you no choice.

So go down the road. Be death, be stardust, enter
the duality known to the generations who are vanished,
who left behind this double image, but only half
the message, just the instructions for how to begin.

Angels of the Inquisition

What Hailey wants is a couch to match her nail polish.
What she wants is a little less sunshine every day.
What she *requires* is an actual, measurable reduction
in the golden, buttery, palm-lined, pumped up,
       slicked down,
born again happiness, joy and boundless energy
that rides in all the convertibles gliding down
       Santa Monica Boulevard
as if it were a champagn- colored river of Chablis.
Frank was right, she says, exhaling breath and smoke
       into the Santa Anas,
there's a lot to hate about California. But this isn't
       California, I remind her. It's L.A.

And where else would she live, our little actress, our
       soft-core queen?
Our Lady Chatterly, Godiva, Mindy, Miranda, Aurora,
       Roxanne, Renee?
She is nourished by mission culture, by the angels of
       the Inquisition
who speak Spanish at their meetings in the morning, but
are not quite so Madrileno in their accent when they're
       howling through the Tenderloin at night.
What Hailey wants is for a priest to fall in love with her,
to struggle with his conscience in a room that's full

of orange blossoms and brocade.
What Hailey wants is for a man to defy God while
        standing on an earthquake fault.
What she wants is for something to start all over
        again, something new.

What I need is for my frequent flyer miles to get me
        someplace cooler.
This is brush fire season, crazy time. Hailey wants to
        drive to Tijuana, Matamoros.
She wants to make her kind of movies with a gaucho:
Don Diego, rape and pillage in the burning time
I call America West from every Chinese restaurant on Sunset
but they are having bomb scares: flights are canceled,
        trips are delayed.
Outside, the oceans are rising, mission bells are tolling,
        conquistadors are galloping up the coast
What Hailey wants is Cuervo Gold and limes on a
        veranda, lots of money, lots of time.
What she wants is what she needs, and los angelinos
        will provide it,
those madonnas of the rack and whip, those beauties,
those terrors, who knew from the beginning that they
        would bring us to our knees.

Arkhangelsk

Oh little sister, far from home, far from the frozen herring and the
       rusting submarines
We will give you wine instead of vodka. We will show you
       the Atlantic, wider yet than the cold White Sea.
And we will be your comrades, we will dance on May Day,
       wear red scarves with all our outfits.
We will serve black bread with all our hearty soups.

Little sister, we always knew that you would make this journey.
Girls at the playground, girls at formal dances, at our weddings
       and in our homes.
We always knew that you would join us. We kept a place for you
       to hang your coat, to dry your gloves.
And while you rest, we will stand guard. We will pound grain
       into a feast for you
And speak your name in all our prayers.

Nations are dying, little sister. Fields are left unplowed
       and cattle wander rutted roadsm
But when the sky has lowered to the earth and you have seen
       the archangel rising from the sea, the ice,
Do not fear him, little sister, do not sell yourself to pay his price.
For we are some of many, we are the first of waves of women,
       we are the generations

born to carry you across the frontier that sometimes appears at
        the edge of history,
the silver line drawn by the ancestors when their hearts
        were still shaped like knives.

Our Post-Soviet History Unfolds

This is what she says about Russia, in the year 2000, in
a restaurant on Prince Street, late on a summer night.
She says: *All the chandeliers were broken and in the winter,*
you couldn't get a drink, not even that piss from Finland.
The whole country was going crazy. She thinks she is speaking
about the days before she left, but I think, actually, that she is
recounting history. Somebody should be writing all this down.

Or not. Perhaps the transition from Communism to a post-Soviet
federation as seen through the eyes of a woman who was hoping,
at least, for an influx of French cosmetics is of interest only to me.
And why not? It seems that the fall of a great empire—revolution!
murder! famine! martial music!—has had a personal effect.
Picture an old movie: Here is the spinning globe, the dotted line
moving, dash by dash, from Moscow across the ocean to
New York and it's headed straight for me. Another blonde
with an accent: the city's full of them. *Nostrovya!* A toast
to how often I don't know what's coming at me next.

So here is a list of what she left behind: a husband, an abortion,
a mathematical education, and a black-market career in
trading currencies. And what she brought: a gray poodle,
eight dresses, and a fearful combination of hope, sarcasm,
and steel-eyed desire to which I have surrendered. And now
I know her secrets: She will never give up smoking.

15

She would have crawled across Eastern Europe and fed
that dog her own blood if she had to. And her mother's secrets:
she would have thought, at last, that you were safe with me.
She hated men. Let me, then, acknowledge that last generation
of the women of the enemy: They are a mystery to me.
They would be a mystery even to my most liberal-minded friends.

That's not to say that the daughter, this new democrat, can't be
a handful. And sometimes noisy: One of those girls you see
now (ice-blue manicure, real diamonds, and lots of DKNY)
leans over from the next table and says, *Can't you ask your wife
to hold it down?* My wife? I suppose I should be insulted,
but I think it's funny. This is a dangerous woman they want
to quiet here. A woman who could sew gold into the ragged lining
of anybody's coffin. Who knows that money does buy freedom.
Who just this morning has obtained a cell phone with a bonus plan.
She has it with her, and I believe she means to use it.
Soon, she will be calling everyone, just to wake them up.

The Causeway

Come near. The day is closing down. Dinner is
burning, the eternal is proving to be temporary, the
divine is showing signs of being cruel. So come near.

Talk to me.
And as you do,
because you do,

a car crosses the causeway, coming home. Human
beings, expelled from their beds in the morning—
tired people, who have made very little money—
are walking across the causeway, coming home.
The animals who were loyal to them are coming
home. Birds flock here, dreams, slave generations
still chained to their overwhelming sacrifice are
dragging themselves across the causeway, coming
home. The last survivors are coming home. Love,
wounded and weary; love with its few remaining
followers, its bag of candles and threadbare
dancing shoes, takes one last look back as it crosses
the causeway, coming home. The ghosts of those
who thought that they would never get here
are here now, on the causeway, coming home.

And the day is closing down.
So come near.
Talk to me.
And as you do,
because you do,

aching decades of labor and struggle begin to
climb down from their machines and even I,
skilled with my tools, proud of my weapons,
allow that it may be time to lay down these
great endeavors and come home. Oh how long
we have all traveled and how far to set just
this first footfall upon your sacred promise
that in the evening, there would be a bridge.

Why We Took the Coastal Evacuation Route

We took our souvenirs and our unemployment checks.
We took our interest in the Kennedy assassination
and our misguided careers. We took snacks. We took
our x-rays, our drugs, and our best costumes. We took
our troubled past. We took our unfinished projects,
we took money, we took tools. And we took the pets,
who looked worried up until the last minute. Then we
took the coastal evacuation route, driving all night until
we found a place to stop and figure out what's next.
But that should be clear soon, because out here, when
you turn on the radio, instead of music you hear boats
whispering to each other. Big ones and little ones,
lining up behind the breakwater, waiting for their
chance to sail away. What do they know? Where are
they going? The pets are working together to adjust our
antenna and we expect to be the first to hear the news.

The Mayans

The scowl is caught in jadeite.
The flattened face on a green bead
displayed in the orchestral light of the museum
also boards the train on Steinway Street.
The warriors are going to the factories.
They sew and sew, these little people.
They sew themselves into oblivion
while our health towers over them.
Our honey, our nutritious breads, our Europe.

I say that history is a heavy stone in that museum,
A golden block that nobody can move.
It is the weight that locks the ossuary,
The brute strength of the altar stone in fine Italian chapels.
It breaks the sword of every century, splitting the jewels like candy
that even starving children are afraid to eat.

I say that all of history is frightening. It deserves
to be boxed up and viewed from behind steel chains.
For think of this: how history has harmed us.
Think how it will not change.
For every kindness we have paid with an extinction.
See that star exploding? It is history, hammering at our heads.

So kings, princes, eaters of hearts—
This is what I want to ask you:
If our Christ were reborn and walked among us
whispering that last secret into our fearful ears,
would you be beaten? Would you submit?
Or could you find your way back to the ball courts,
restore the ruined planetarium,
and calculate, from sacred zero,
all the formulas time has denied?

Little Mayans, European blondes—
let us follow the route of the thunderbird that
flies before the storm,
Let us toss the ball,
Let us outwit history,
At last, at last, let our game begin,

Jews in Nashville

Surprisingly, we were simpatico. We understood the
modest skyline and the bus routes that took the workers
to their modest jobs. We loved the catfish sandwiches!
And the bitter countryside reminded us of the years
when there was no harvest and the people mourned.
We know any number of stories that are flattering to
all denominations, and we traded these for visits to
private homes, where we were not mocked. Instead,

we were invited to walk the roads out to the orchards
and the graveyards. We were given access to family
photos and took copious notes. We walked respectfully
along the banks of the river that had agreed to lend both
commerce and recreation to the city and then we shared
the secrets of a people who are largely misunderstood:
Like you, they told us, *we revere the ones who God has
driven crazy. And when He breaks our hearts, we keep the
secret to ourselves. We eat our bread and save our money
for the upkeep of our wives and children, who adore us.
Sometimes, for no reason, we stomp around with joy.*

That is to say, when we were younger, we thought that
travel would enlighten us. That cities were connected by

the music on the radio. We thought that Jews were
welcome everywhere and that anyone who had a
history was ready to put down their guns and dance.

The Single-Killer Theory

It is a warm winter. The diplomats are overdressed and
the young duchess won't come out of her air-conditioned
Hummer. Why should she? What she wants is hip-hop.
What she wants is underground and Japanese. She couldn't
care less about who triumphs in the current negotiations. In
certain circles, they think her boredom is a protest for peace.

Meanwhile, I'm still worried about the assassination. I think
it was lonely Oswald, but that leaves me out on a limb with
Norman Mailer. *Dear Norman: I agree that his return to New
Orleans may be a red herring, as was his trip to Mexico and
the famous photo in the backyard. Still, I am troubled by
new evidence.* Norman does not write back. Without
his endorsement, how will I get my book deal, or funding
for my documentary? Even my Guggenheim is on hold.

Time is killing me; events run on. First, war descends, then
aliens play peek-a-boo with their big faces peeping around the
corner of the moon. Tickets arrive for Burning Man, for the
inauguration, the protest, the wedding of the year. And at the
office, the backlog is getting worse: I stamp papers for the
boss as he denies all claims and grabs mercy by the throat
because the county wants him to. The county is our master
but even they don't seem to know who they are working for.

Finally, a letter arrives without a postmark. It says:

Keep up the good work. You may be on to something with this single-killer theory. Remember, he only claimed to be a patsy.

Living with the Red Menace

The Red Menace used to live upstairs from me
This was in the Bronx, on the Grand Concourse,
        in the spring of 1953.
Everyone was afraid of him but I could relate to his
inner child (agrarian reform) and so we got along.
We used to read Ferlinghetti together—remember, the
Red Menace was something of a rebel once—and go
to Yankee games (presaging his Cuban phase: both he
        and Castro were crazy about baseball).
He felt bad about the blacklist and missed his days
in Hollywood—what a comedown for him, living
        among Poles and Czechs!
(Refugees from simple satellite countries, no less.)
But he still retained a fondness for Jews, which caused
no end of trouble later: one more decade and all you
had to do was say "fellow traveler" in front of a rabbi,
        and he'd faint dead away.

And was he a talker, that Red Menace! We'd sit for hours
        on the fire escape
(just like in *West Side Story)* and he'd go on and on about
celebrities he had known: Lenin, Anastasia, General
        Zukhov—you wouldn't think it,
but apparently they all had a lighter side. And he liked
to speculate about collectives, though he focused more on

the unconscious than on five-year plans.
This was during his spiritual period, when he decided
to make pilgrimages to far-away countries, which always
        turned out badly for them.
(He was a user, I have to admit that, and for all his
fancy philosophy, he really didn't know how to share)
Then there was that night in '57 that he threw the
        Sputnik party.
Of course, no one came, but the Red Menace was
        in his glory.
He munched on deli sandwiches and speculated on
the bright promise of the future. *Beep, beep beep,*
        his ham radio replied.

Now, of course, he's just a shadow of his former self.
I still visit him occasionally at the King David nursing home
        in West Orange, New Jersey.
(Yes, the Jews again—when they heard how far he'd fallen,
        they felt sorry for him
and took him in.) Sometimes his mind wanders and he thinks
        he's on the phone to Mao
(whom he detested: Kruschev, he said, at least had a sense
        of humor).
But mostly, he just sits in his wheelchair and drinks tea.
Oh, he still gets mail and the occasional student comes

to see him, but otherwise, he seems to have lost interest
in the outside world.
If he dies, he wants to be buried near Los Alamos.
Now those were tricksters, he says, *idealists—they knew
how to invent death and sell it to the common man.*
But that's just the cynic in him talking: we were always
smarter than that. When we wanted to, we were perfectly
capable of giving it away for free.

Women in Business

The pretty Chinese girl in Ferragamo shoes is here to sell me large-format color prints with velcro backing. I need these things for a business event, which will not be described for the purpose of this story. But here's the scene: we are in my office. Nice chairs, nice desk, nice view of glass towers and a stone cathedral. For a while, we do some techno talk: the possibility of dot gain, the nature of moires. But because I know this girl a little, because we have established what we will give and what we'll take in the course of making sales, when I see that her mind is wandering and her hand, maybe, is shaking, I can say, *What's wrong, Miranda?* and she tells me. Oh boy, is she ready to talk.

But not here. So ten minutes later, at two-thirty on a cold spring afternoon, we are sitting in a bar on Second Avenue. Little blue lamps on the tables, orange lamps on the polished bar. We think about wine, but then, the hell with it, we order lemon Stoli. The hell with the rest of the afternoon. And so here's the story: her ex-boyfriend has palmed a key and trashed her apartment. Wrecked the stereo, punched the iMac, looted all the coordinates from Ikea, and peed in her dresser drawers. Her cat is hiding in the splinters and will not come when called. What's wrong with her, she asks, that she thought the boyfriend could be a husband? *Or rather,* she says, *I guess I should be asking, what's wrong with men?*

Ah well. Broaching that subject calls for at least three more drinks
Since we both have brothers that we hold in high esteem, we agree
that we cannot condemn the gender as a whole. Then she mentions
Jersey boys, those beauties in bandannas ruined by fate and rock
and roll. And Spanish boys, too hot, too sensitive. Even in winter,
the fruits of the Caribbean are the meal that they will feed to your
desire. But Miranda is still dreaming. And me? I decide to let my
guard down, to confess my real problem (I mean, beyond my
limited budget for the event): that lately, I have grown nostalgic for
an old identity, for someone who unexpectedly kissed me in a
hallway twenty years ago. For Eastham and Provincetown. For
cold sheets and a Portuguese tide. *Oh, I always knew that,*
Miranda says. *What did you think you were trying to hide?*

So what happens next? I get a discount on my color prints.
Miranda goes home to clean her house and find her cat.
And the next day and the next day, we return to work,
for such is the nature of women in business, of the years
spent in the office, watching sun and shadow pass along
the ledges of the stone cathedral: to trade clues in conversation
even as we conduct a fair transaction. Even as the headache
builds, the lover leaves: to sell each other hope.

Tales of the Mohawk Valley

The old cities are coming back to life again: Oneida, Utica,
       Syracuse, Ilion.
Their motto of service and industry has replaced even the
extremes of upstate weather as the topic of conversation on
       everyone's lips.
Brickfaces have been repointed, geraniums snapped into
       new window boxes,
and the papers have added food columns and sections on
       the arts.
The spirit is municipal, the worship, Presbyterian, and everyone
is busy, busy, busy—even prayer is jobbed out for a purpose:
Keep the frost off the asparagus, the trout eager for
       the sportsman's hook.
In the summer, contented people fall asleep in Adirondack chairs
and their dreams are scented by valley crops and hilltop flowers.

But in your mother's house on Eller Street, with Canada
       in the window,
the wind sweeps in, already thinking about winter. This is
the Leatherstocking wind that closed the old factories, that
brings the headless horseman and blows witches into the yard
       to steal our housecoats from the line.
And in your mother's house on Eller Street, progress has not
       reached us:
I sleep too much and you have managed to remain unemployed.

Every afternoon, the pots and pans bang out their grief: who will
        make our stew,
who will pour out the batter for our flapjacks? Every night,
the house weeps and refuses to be sold. Every morning,
I try to make it to the store, and every street is like a bridge
        across a mill basin,
and the mill wheel is turning and we are the labor of its years,
        the poor grist.

So come. If the house will not join with the community, just
        lock the door and walk away.
We can cross the Mohawk Valley while the seasons are
        still turning,
walk beneath the waterfalls, across great tables of broken schist
to where the earth has cleaved open and peer into its iron heart,
        its silver veins.
At the end of the valley there is a lake with a monster who lives
        in a deep, cold pool.
That can be our destination. We can buy a guidebook and
        some chocolate
and picnic on the shore. Thus will we partake of the bounty
        of the state,
participate in its rejuvenation. We will blend in with the
tourists, be indistinguishable from people with money and
        plans and things to do.

We will ride a boat that glides above the monster's house and speculate with strangers: *How do you think he makes his living? How has he survived so long, unknown, unseen, and free?*

The Traveler's News

On the plane back from Morocco, we blamed ten years of
rock and reggae, and cold winters in the Haight for the idea
that Marrakesh would be the playhouse where we could
hide out from an evil time. But that was over, so we hopped
the jet stream back to Cali and hunkered down in the
Hollywood Hills. The jo- fair girls sent us to offices; the

work paid for nights on the Strip: canned soup and aspirin
in the evening, cigarettes at five a.m. to feed the thin hope
that lodged itself behind the breastbone. The thin days that
wrestled with us, always gaining ground. But we took
it all: we lived the life and used ourselves before we learned

to use our money. We watched what happened until we finally
caught on: there is no evidence of a conspiracy. The world is
just the world despite the fact that it resists us. Despite the fact
that it still displays its ancient jewelry and mausoleums but
will not divulge their source. The world remakes us, but
that is automatic. Otherwise, it does not sleep. It does not

dream. It is neither for us nor against us. It is not a theory
and not a game, though it changes in the middle; at the
end, it is never the same. But that's the news that travelers
hear, the teaching edge we've learned to walk, the
broken road that only heals itself the farther on you go.

The Bondage Club

In the morning we put on our sharp blue suits and
go to hear the delegates speak through broken teeth.
These are the women whose names the press must be
cautioned not to mention, the ones who smuggle food
across warring borders, drive defiant crosses into the
burning ground. We give them our attention, we
write them checks. And yet we are not ashamed to
live here in our bounty. It is ours. It is what we have.

In the evening, you put on your black, your gold, and
go out to the bondage club. Little thing that you are, I
understand the need to slap someone around. The need
for photographs and scars. And you say these are the nicest
people you've ever met: they're just in pain (oh yes, a little
joke: I refer to the physical as well as the psychic). Little
thing that you are, come home when you have had enough.
I will apply the universal remedy. Perhaps serve tea.

And when the next day comes around, I'll be the bad
girl. You go to work, I'll hit the bars. Let's put it this
way: peace is impossible, violence endemic, guilt the
natural foundation of our lives. *Our* lives. Oh, the years
I spent researching magical solutions! Page 309: *In
the moonlight, in a bloody dance.* We could try that,
too. It won't work, but it might be our kind of fun.

Rogue states, rogue lives: all women suffer. All women
search the empty marketplace, live on morsels, learn to
be light sleepers in uneasy beds. Little thing that you are,
pay the madman and apologize for nothing: No matter what
you do, the years rage on through all their seasons of pain;
I will be satisfied when you are satisfied, which means that
I must watch you take your chances. Save you from all
the ghosts and ancestors who think there is another way.

Big Girls

The sun shines all through Sunday. It's a juicy afternoon,
all peachy and sweet. Gulf dreams hit the sweat-stained
walls like margaritas flying off the bar. Did you think
the South was just a game we were playing? A Yankee vacation?
Ballcaps, beer stops, catfish between the bread. Blacker
than the East, more religious than the West, and big girls everywhere.

Big girls. Like to knock you down, like to date you, talk
your ear off night and day, then hand you a baby, a dog,
and a bag of groceries and before you know it, you're married to it,
like the rest of us, saying *yessur* to our own dear Christ
crooning on the radio, living down the road, down a ways,
living in multicultural bliss. Just the mention of snacks

can bring us together: popems, cruellers, fritters and eclairs
crusted with pink-y sprinkles, plus red, white, and blue on the happy
holidays. When the neighbors gather, English is optional:
Did I tell you this story in Hmong, patois, Mexicali; in this story,
no one dies, we all behave, and we don't need money

and the big girl, my girl, big as a house crusher, a democracy,
big as the world blessed by salvation, beaming with love.

Starina

I don't want to live in the city anymore, with its
skullcaps and killers and girls from the personals
who are too young for me. Starina, Starina,
I don't want to climb your stairs anymore because
I don't care: when there was incense, yes, and radio
and hash and we could walk in the cold on East
10th Street in our little shirts, our little scarves.
And boots that said to hell with everything, you
with your Egyptian rings and your wild hair.

I don't want to go to work anymore, because
the world is not a better place. You in your long
dress, straddling the rows, planting peppers:
I am disappointed in you, in the commune and
the community. Blah, blah, blah all day on the
phone: is this what you trained me for? All that
unusual sex, all that howling at the moon. It left
me tired, Starina. But it left me needing more.

So I don't want to cooperate for even one more day.
Been there, done that and I don't see the point.
I miss you all and I despise you: how unkind it was
of you to teach me to think for myself. About art
and literature. About human rights and women.
About the struggle, which in some corner of the mind

goes on and on. You should have written a steal-this
manual for when the show was over. You should
have explained how to melt back into the crowd.

But I won't do it, not by a long shot. Soon I'll be
marching to the luncheonette with the other angry
elderly, where I will munch my cheese sandwich and
foment plans to vote everybody out. You, too, Starina,
now that you've grown fat and wicked. Now that
you refuse to change your ways. Remember the big
yellow dog I found that you told me belonged to
everybody? Well, he's old now, too, and angry, and
living here with me. Any minute, I'm going to let him

loose into the world to remind you how the animal
always comes back to haunt us and how the new
days are just the old days, starting right about now.

Mountain Lakes

Now do you believe that we are out of harm's way?
Having made the pilgrimage through the Holland Tunnel
we are old enough, in fact, long overdue in this bare suburb.
The house imagines that we are any couple moving in.
It presents March robins, throws stones, thinking they
are windy flowers. We have purchased this blindness,
used your mother's money. The last trip she didn't make
to Europe has brought us to New Jersey, to this town where
there is no mountain, no plurality of lakes. And thus it is a
perfect painting: an illusion into which, slowly, we progress.

On the first day I give you the kitchen: linoleum, ice-cream
chairs, Fiestaware. You are the blonde here, and fortunate.
Creamy cakes and fat pies will bake up in the strong
seasons of your heart. I prowl the corridors
of light and shadow, stunned by the long gray days,
stunned by the silence of the morning. Now,
having come and gone a thousand times, having done
everything I thought I could, I finally settle on the
red sofa, the color old and plush, from a Hopper print.
You walk in carrying a tray of sandwiches. We recognize
each other. And I wonder: do you still love me? Still
practice that old trick of being both merciless and kind?

The Little Dog Dance

As we cross the square, she remarks that it has been
a warm December—first we had ice cream at Thanksgiving
and there are still flowers in the park. And I agree.
Everything is so unusual this year!
The talk turns again to holidays. In Odessa,
she waited for Father Christmas and then toasted him
with tea. But everything is different here—pilgrims,
pumpkins, popcorn on the trees. She tells me
that her mother's Christmas story was the Romanovs
and she still knows the names of all the sisters.
She knows that Anastasia did not get away.

Now she lives in a city where we claim
it hasn't snowed since we were children.
And this year, it seems like summer never left!
The sparrows in the park are as happy as parakeets.
My little dog spins across the cobblestones.
Each leaf could be a harbinger of joy!
There is the scent of fruit and woodsmoke in the air.
The breezes float like scarves around the trees.
So many seasons are caught in those golden branches!
I whistle for the dog, who always knows
how to find me. Behind us, winter is just
the ghost that follows as we turn for home.

This year, peculiar currents assail the globe: riptides,
ebb tides, blue moons out of phase. Yet Nonya
is serene. She has seen rifles floating in the bloody
river and grandmas sweeping the streets with twigs.
Clearly there are calamities enough without interpreting
the stars. We have learned enough about fate and its
preposterous measures, about escaping from what
has been left behind: there is the little room in Odessa,
the little room in New York. What is the difference?
Only that here we are happy! In this new city,
we have good jobs, TV, each other, and even in
the strangest weather, all the little dogs still dance.

Late at Night, in a Beach Town

Summer. Late at night. The ocean is in the air, tangy
with the smell of wandering. On the shortwave, there is the voice
of an American living in Brazil, reading the names of people
who have sent him letters because they heard his broadcast.
That's it; that's all: *Hello, this is Gabriel. I picked up your*
program one night in Yorba Linda. In the next room,
you are broadcasting dreams: lately, it's been your father,
who was a disappointment, whose disappearing act ended
with his dying on my father's birthday, leaving us
with the burden of symbolism. It's an interesting but unwanted gift.

Summer. Late at night. Honey, I am restless. I don't know
what I want and no one can help me. By the light of the little
plastic lighthouse lamp the past has taken to reappearing:
my parents, my mistakes, my glimpse of freedom, my career.
Honey, you do your best for me but I am drifting further
and further away. *Hello, this is Amarylis, Bertie, Diego, Garson,*
Frances, Alan, Pauline, Paulette. The names are pushed
through an antenna, shot into the canyons of the sky,
and fly back to America. Inside my radio, my own black box,
they have a minute to live. Less. And then they're gone.

Do you know that I can remember every radio
I ever owned and tell you where I got it? I won one
on the boardwalk, bought another in the psychedelic days.

Music, voices, wandering signals—late at night, I try
to sort through the things that are important, but I am not sure.
Little details overwhelm the big events. Years are
remembered only by their songs. What happens next?
Where are we going? In the bedroom, you are swimming
back from the land that has trapped your angry father.
Breakfast is thinking about making itself. And for the rest
of the night, the radio continues to say hello.

Missing Person

They wrote about it in the newspaper: how I
hung up on the woman who called and said,
I have found the body of your missing sister
because I didn't believe there is a place called Blue Earth,
Minnesota. Because I am no longer related
to my sister. Because I do not care for
these kind of mysteries and I do not invite
      old ghosts into my house.

But of course that wasn't the end of it.
My brother checked the map of Minnesota.
He had men dispatched to investigate the story,
which involves a pickup on a rainy highway,
a murder, a dead girl without a name,
an unmarked grave, a set of dental charts,
a Midwestern mom who decided to be
a forensic detective. Thank you to the TV
and movie industry for suggesting
that in modern times, everyone can
      and should be found.

Here is the truth: she was a stepsister.
We couldn't stand her. She was disturbed
and dangerous: angry, medicated, mean. And she was
also a girl, a human, a sweet baby once,

someone who knew her told me. She liked the Beatles,
        she had a talent for art,

and in 1979, she got up in the middle of the night
and walked off into oblivion. They wrote about it
in the newspaper: *No trace was ever found.*
Now we await the DNA results and dream
about graveside visits, court-ordered exhumations,
and tell each other, *Daddy would want us to find out.*
Late at night, we call each other, hooking into the power
grid, the billion zillion volts that hum between
D.C. and New York, to ask again, *How much,*
        really, do you remember?

as if we were doing this only by dead reckoning,
also lost and crazy, or else as partners in whatever
        turns out to have been the crime.

Someone Like You

Steam-heated rooms, winter, and your thin arms
waving away everyone you were accused of loving.
That's how I remember you: blonde as the girls
of tomorrow and mean to everyone. In and out
of the shops on Cornelia Street to buy your cake
and cigarettes, in and out of the boys' bars,
other women's lives—the days went on and on
like that. The years. There was light in the
background but it was dim and dangerous, like
a far-off fire in an oilfield. Like the aftermath of war.

It should have been a disaster, the kind of life
that I led then. The life in which I wanted
someone like you. Instead, when we met again
one night in the no-name town where we grew up,
no one seemed surprised. You said, *So, sister,*
I hear you got a job. You're making money.
Why don't you tell your mother that you won't be home?

Two hours later, in a hotel on the Jersey Turnpike,
I said that you could bite and you could scream
and you could tell me everything that anyone
had ever done to you and I wouldn't falter,
I wouldn't feel a thing, since I had wised up
to the fact that some women want to see

how much it really takes to kill them;
some women know the answer in advance.

So in the morning, we woke up without our
girl disguises and left it all behind us: the crimes
that we committed, the sex we thought was
owed us, the razors and the garnets that we wore
when we were those creatures, that generation,
the kind of lovers who crave the taste of blood.

About Patti Boyd and Me

Here is the Figaro. A block away, the old mob neighborhood
is hunched down against the rain. Hard cookies and pistachios
lean into the window. Tap on the glass and old women start baking:
hard cakes, hard loaves. This morning, I came to MacDougal Street
to buy a ring, and now I can't seem to leave.
Thirty years ago, Patti, this is what I thought was home.

There is a picture of you on a train in 1967: a thin girl with
long hair on her way to see the Mahareshi. I was a thin girl
with long hair, on her way to buy hashish. I had on too much silver,
and I was wild and sick in those days, when you had all that
mod chic and rocker style. When you had those young eyes:
living on the edge of everyone else's life, you probably
devised the best solution: Marry. Marry well.

I hear you live in the Apennines now, or travel constantly.
That's what I learned, too, from my course in meditation,
though the goal was not peace but movement: this was
a bad city then, and you had to play it, you had to
just open the door and run. I'm not complaining, Patti:
I survived it. I ate it when I had to, liked it when they said to.
I killed it when there was nothing else to do.

But silver wears down. And even pretty girls get lonely;
even crazy girls want to stop. Because silver wears down

when it's supposed to. Because I can still name all the dramas
I appeared in on the nights, the days that rolled away from me
between Renwick Street and the Chelsea Hotel.

And now I think that silver wears down when it decides to.
Last week I saw a picture of you in an Italian airport:
scarves and sunglasses and yellow hair. I'm glad to see
you still have a destination. I'm glad the photographers still know
who you are. And me? I bought the ring, I made a call to say
that I was coming home. Me? I fell in love long past the time
I had expected to. I have a dog, a view of the city.
Thanks for asking, Patti. It's a surprise, but I'm doing well.

The Weight of Experience

Crossing the wet fields on a winter afternoon,
the brown rows oozing nutrients and seeds,
I see the house at the edge of a crossroads. Our house,
built on the beds of frozen vegetables, a system
of roots and rivers, pumpkin vines. These were the years
when I was expected to fight the weather
and you played the part of the blonde from witch country,
the beauty with an illness, a premonition.
This was in the land of gorges, of meltwater
and giants, where I was happy to stand between you
and the elements, to work, to bring home the food.
I walked the roads through every season;
I mastered the wind. Remember: in this life, I was young.
I loved you. I was capable of anything.

Now, I turn the corner onto a sand street,
toward another house, set deep in permanent summer.
The bluest sky, the dunes like walls. I am followed
by a blind sun as I cross this valley of silica and fine-ground glass.
All the windows, too, are blinded, all the gardens
claimed by the beach. I have spent the day in an office;
I have traveled here by train, in my writer's suit, carrying
the pens that still inscribe your name, only your name.
This is the longest I have believed in anything. This is
the life in which no one knows how old I am. This life,

this life, these final years, when you still remember
to turn me out into the world. When the weight of experience
grows lighter with each step I take and you are
always waiting, the blonde behind the open door.

I Have Thought Enough

in memory of Donald Barthelme

I have spent enough long nights wired into the *om*.
I have thought enough about departed blondes and
heroines. I have remembered everything I ever
want to: all I'm keeping is an afternoon with the
famous author who threw open his closet and said,
Well, there's my archives, dearie. If there's
       a fire, I'm going out for a drink.

Which became my famous story, my excuse:
A writer told me before he died. That was in
New York; in California, you were riding
on the windy roads, high in the clouds, going
into the city, coming home. What kind of life
could it have been, starting over ever day?
There was something you must have had in mind,
driving east from the dry desert, something
that you thought would turn out better
       in the cold.

Is what you found out, instead, that I am difficult
and not romantic? On a French island, I walked
you through an empty prison owned by seabirds.
In Mexico, I drank the water and squandered money.
I bought you dresses and horses, but never wrote

the book you wanted. I did what I wanted and
wrote about it in my letters: *Burn the archives
and run away with me.*

And so you did. Now in the morning, whoever
wakes first opens the door to let in the weather of
a new country. To see if the way is open. If the
coast is clear. If not, we make some sandwiches
and watch a movie. But if there is a chance, then
we will choose each other all over again before we
slip away. Which must have been what he meant
to tell me, what you really had in mind when you
gunned the engine and drove, without a blindfold,
straight into these dangerous days.

There is a Woman Standing on a Terrace

There is a woman standing on a terrace. She is
wearing a silk sheath—green I think; as pale as
tea. She is holding a drink so icy that it tastes
like mercury. The Pleiades are overhead and she
is gazing eastward, toward the South China Sea.

How do you know? Because this is after
After all your work is done, after the passing of
so many, the travel that took you nowhere.
After you married and divorced, after your children
defied you, which meant that you had done your job.

Now you are so old that you are free to hope.
Nothing needs to be considered except the root
of your desire, which has become that
crystal sliver of pain that all the doctors told you
was a chronic headache but you suspect might be
the original nerve still pulsing, the ache
that has been with you, always.

So eat breakfast. Pack lightly. Then start your journey
to the deep water city, to the hotel on a hill above Repulse Bay.
What does it matter that you were "never meant to be here?"
What does it matter that when you speak to her she
will answer in French? You will be able to understand her

if you want to and she will know who you are.
Bring her a drink that tastes of melon. And as the sky
hangs out its starry animals—a fish, a bear,
a canny dog—tell her how long it took to form
these constellations. That human beings have named them.
That anything is possible and you, you are the proof.

The Drought Summer

Newburgh, New York, 1970

It's hotter than it's ever been, says the announcer.
I trust the TV, so begin to worry that this might be
like one of those old movies where the earth
stands still and fireballs rain down from the sky.
Huge, overheated dinosaurs could climb out of
great cracks in the earth and knock down our house.
Oh for God's sake, you sigh. *Why are you so
morbid? Turn off the television and let's go out.*

Our neighbor is in his lettuce field and you decide
that we should help him water. Our dogs go off
to chase wild peahens in the meadows
as we set up the irrigators: silver wheels that
span the rows of tender Butterheads and Salinas.
Like little green brains already plotting to avoid
the dinner table, these baby salads drink their
cocktail of spinning water, chemicals and old
radiation leeched from the soil. They could be
bits of jade scattered in this thirsty field. They
could be thinking about how to poison us all.

For lunch we have sandwiches and sun tea,
sunshine, no rain in sight; the woods beyond
the barn are dry as tinder. We listen to

the crop report and hear that most of the countryside
is suffering; twigs, grass, soil, all crackle underfoot.
This is getting pretty bad, our neighbor says,
by August, even the witches will be hauling water.
And I, of course, want to know *What witches?*
But you've had enough of this now, and push me
down the porch, across the road, toward home.

I should be writing, you should be in your
workshop, but it's too hot to even think
In the evening, we drive across the county to a fair.
At the nickel pitch I meet our neighbor's son
and ask him about the witches. *I saw one once,*
he tells me, *in the woods. I threw a rock at her.*

Later, as I'm riding the Ferris wheel,
as I'm lifted into the deep, mysterious, blue-black,
star-encrusted sky, I see you down below,
at a farm stand, inspecting cans of peaches,
beans and beets that have miraculously survived
the drought summer. And because I see that you are
confidently planning for the fall, it seems possible for me
to hope for the future that you believe in, or at least
to borrow it from you, one small, neighborly handful at a time.

Timeless Canyon

In the great quiet here. In the wind that searches the lost pueblo
and moves on. In the clouds that gather above the flat mountains
In the heaviness of the air, in the threat of rain that never comes.
In the darkness of the bedroom, in the shadow on the clock.
In the sight of you floating in a blue tile pool in an old desert.
In the many ways I've come here, in the lateness of the afternoon.

In the asking, in the telling. And above, beneath, beyond.
In the jewel that you have hidden in a secret, in the secret that
you keep. In the great quiet here. I set a chair beside the pool
but cannot occupy its space. Cannot. Which is why I followed
you: to learn how to enter the world. To learn the mysterious
way through many canyons. In the timeless time, in the deepest
blue. Will you be the one to ask me, order me to rest?

*Rest. The clouds cannot escape the mountains. The rain
will never come.* In the great quiet here. In the wind that
searches the lost pueblo. In the impact crater, scattered with
jewels. In the night that is falling, in the bedroom where we
will sleep. In the name that I will call you, in the name that
you have given me. In the footprints on the tile, in the pitcher
by the bed. In the sight of you, drinking from a glass of still water.
In the time until the impact. And above, beneath, beyond.

Dear Mary, I Am Out West

What I should write to you about is Santa Fe,
so hot beneath its Christian cowboy sun, each day
resurrected in a desert that yields up gardens and
paintings, architecture baked by touring artists at
great expense. There is light here, all day, everywhere:
it shimmers and sweats and is as weighty as gold,
which is its color. Women smile with golden faces,
they pay with gold for golden dresses. Do you get
the picture? Add me, in snakeskin boots, buying a

tiny portrait of a thunderbird, a totem that will fly me
all the way to California. Dear Mary: I am out West.
I should be sending postcards, so here is yours: I am
traveling the golden miles but want to come home.
I need a little rain; I need cool sheets all flowery with
soon-it's-April, the salt wind blowing down from
Nova Scotia to our own cold shore. Meet me in
Truro, meet me in a bar where everyone is growing

old and happy. Meet me where white winter light
melts into silver on the tables and twilight falling
on the ocean beyond the window contains everything
that we remember. Meet me where there is cake
and wine. Meet me: in the short time left, there is

nothing more important than the beloved place,
the single afternoon, the going back, the knowing
when, and who to wait for at the evening door.

We're Ready in Roswell

Well, you have to have these things, these unexplained events.
Something has to come crashing out of the sky once in a while
or else we'd have nothing to think about except what to make
        for lunch.
Personally, I'd still be wandering the aisles of the Food Lion
staring blankly at the cans of peas, if it wasn't for Roswell.
Liquid metal debris, alien hieroglyphics, ranch hands
        threatened by the government—
I love it all! I love Area 51! And reverse engineering of
    off-world technology!
(There are whole chunks of my recent past that could use
        a touch of that.)
I mean, think about it: don't you want to believe that there's
more going on here than what meets our beady little eyes?

And what if there is? What if you walk out into the desert
        one night
and look up in the sky, only to find that one of those
oscillating lights isn't really a charter flight to Vegas?
Or say you sit down on the hard-scrubbed ground and
        jeepers creepers,
do you feel that hum, that vibe that says there's something
        out there,
something big and strange and itching to make contact.

Then what do you do? That's easy! Just fax us here at
      the Little Ale'e'in.
We're out here on the highway, ready in New Mexico,
      ready in Rachel.
The cattle are eager to be mutilated! Crop circles are
      springing up,
even in our tiny gardens! We've got Sat Phones and
Geiger counters, plenty of drinking water and maps of
      every quadrant of the sky.
We're here, we're hoping and we're happy. We're baking
sheet cakes for the visitors (and hoping they like chocolate).
Even the mayor, a former skeptic who keeps his veggies
      in a pyramid, is making extra soup!

Why We Need to Start a Dialogue

Where are You? Apparently not stuffed into the basket
of chocolate and apples they gave us back in the Bronx,
in the shul-as-small-as-a-box with its golden tassels
and folding chairs—though there are people my age
who still believe that You show up at baseball fields
in the dark winter, carrying a child's soul and the seed
of spring. There are people my age who believe You love
the miscreant, the quiet boys who come out of nowhere
and fight for everything they get. Is that true?

Then what about the girls? Is it okay with you
if we are unsympathetic to pain but spend our whole lives
pretending, helping out so people will say, *What a nice girl,*
and leave us alone to work? Is it okay if all we want to do
is work? What if the rest is unbearable? What if all we remember
is our weeping grandmas who would not love us because love

begets slaughter? And don't forget cancer, which is how
all the grandmas ended up, with Eastern European Nazi
cancer that rammed itself against the liver, cracked bone
with the mad efficiency of a Panzer tank. So what
were You thinking? Chocolate and cancer and unloved
working girls? I hate to tell You this, but there are
people my age who think You are out of Your mind.

And so what if the poets, those straight old men
with their hounds and their teaching degrees,
are standing out in the salt grass on some Christian island,
waiting for You to come in with the tide? Let them wait.
I was talking to You first. People my age are confused
and worried. Clean, bar mitzvahed, but raised
by mothers who smoked and danced and still were

never happy—what did you tell them in the middle
of the night? Did you promise compensation?
Children? But what if they wanted something else?
What if we do? Neither tragedy nor comedy,
but of great consequence, signed by a hand both
fierce and unmistakable, upon a raging sky.

The Anthropic Principle

Two red drinks—pure alcohol, with a maraschino cherry—in
the bar next door, deep in the afternoon. While I hide in my
cool corner, admiring the sawdust and the sides of beef, work
is taking place all over the world: diamonds are being quarried,
slaves are sewing dresses, policemen are loading their rifles,
aiming their guns. As for the rest of us (when we're not
drinking), diligently, we apply ourselves to solving the
problems of the multitudes; diligently, we communicate

our ideas. And here is more to chew on: seventeen rich
grandchildren are coming for lunch tomorrow. Russia awaits,
Africa, the prevention of nuclear war. If I were free, I would
suggest that this is how we do it: more sports, more food.
Certainly, more television. Ducks in funny costumes, wielding
hammers, quacking out a song. That's how we conquered
Communism: the ducks alone brought down the Berlin wall.

So three drinks later, back in the office, I blast fax out my
manifesto, which is simple: we should all relax. Apparently,
no matter what we do, we already do our part; we balance
the cosmological constant just by getting up in the morning
and smacking around our wives. Isn't that amazing! And
here's how it works: according to the anthropic principle,

there could be an infinity of universes: starry bubbles, burning balls, solid boxes of hard time. You name it and they made it: some are gelatinous. Some are inside out. But there is one commonality: none are peopled. None have us. Only the composition of our universe allows for our existence—in fact, our presence is required or the whole thing falls apart. So

here's what I think: what if we all held our breath and stood sideways in a corner so we couldn't be found? Our universe would go wailing through the empty corridors of physics, knocking over furniture and pictures, searching for its vanished friends. Afterward, when we said *Gotcha!* and the universe wept with relief, we could all sit down for a nice cup of something comfy, have a heart-to-heart, and someone, somewhere, might wise up.

Sunset Hammers

When the phone rings in your office, receive the news
as calmly as you would another memo. Another inventory
sheet detailing cost and value. *The price of the goods
we have in stock is fluctuating. The physical integrity
of the materials is of concern.* And as calmly as you
would write an answer *(then stabilize the prices; restate
our faith in the processes and manufacture),* get your
coat and get out the door. Your colleagues will remain

at their stations: behind the business of blue eyes the
phone will go on ringing and must be answered. Even
with faith, with planning, there is just no other way.
And so. Go into the city of tunnels. Of bridges, of
elevated light. Go as a writer, a sailor. Go up the
Mekong, up the Congo, go up the lines of distance
that are laid out like a summons. Go as a visitor,
because in the future, you will be the patient. Go,

because time is getting short, because your dreams
may be prophetic; go because you need to, because
you want to. Go quickly, go now. Already, sunset
hammers at the windows on Mt. Eden Avenue; the
panes burst into red and that vibrato is what you have
begun to hear. Go, because every day there is someplace

you have to be. Work with that feeling. In the end,
nothing else (Get it? *Nada)* may turn out to be true.

Jews in New York

Jews in New York City are circling the comedy clubs,
trying out their punch lines on the neighbors before they
go in. Onstage, Jews are killing the audience, murdering
the assembly. People are laughing so hard that even their
drinks are giggling. Kaluha is in stitches on the floor.
The Jews are doing this so it isn't done to them first.

Jews in New York City are not having an easy time.
They are building harpsichords for the goyim, who play
so beautifully. The Jews shave down the plectrum like
a holy beard, wear wooden roses in their hair, and dance
secret dances with velvet ribbons because they are jealous
of the Christians' sacred music. The Jews are in an uproar
because they are never given any instruments. Their present
is always a tuning fork. Their job is to sound the alarm.

Now the Jews are at the beach, bathing their babies in
the gentle waves. No one knows why the Jews are
attracted to the ocean but this may be what brought
them to New York: its proximity to the future shore.
The Jews indulge in sand and surf; eat ice cream, nap
beneath their striped umbrellas. But they always
keep their hats on so everyone knows how unusual
they are. Then the Jews get on the subway and go

back to the city to run the engines of time. Many have
suspected that this is what they were doing all along.

Jews in New York City like candy in fancy boxes.
They wish they had more money. They are working on
an invention to rid the world of rust. They are thoughtful,
wary and suspicious of God, who returns the favor.
They have called a meeting to discuss their grievances
with Him and plan to begin the proceedings by telling
Him a joke. Soften the old guy up. If he's in a good
mood, maybe he'll start to explain some of this.

Ben Fraker

THE AUTHOR

•

Eleanor Lerman is the author of *The Mystery of Meteors* (2001). She was born in the Bronx, New York, in 1952. She is the author of two other previous books of poetry, published over thirty years ago, *Armed Love* (Wesleyan University Press) and *Come the Sweet By and By* (University of Massachusetts Press), and of a book of short stories, *Observers and Other Stories* (Artemis Press, 2001). After an early, aborted career as a cultural icon (in 1975, *The New York Times* called *Armed Love* "X-Rated" when that was still shocking), she fled the field of art for comedy. She transitioned to true-life crime, working on books with her brother *(No Mercy* and *Public Enemies* by John Walsh with Philip Lerman). She has been nominated for a National Book Award, received the inaugural Juniper Prize, and was the recipient of a fiction grant from the New York Foundation for the Arts. She is a lifelong New Yorker.